In the Footsteps of Explorers

Vasco da Gama

Quest for the Spice Trade

Katharine Bailey

Crabtree Publishing Company

www.crabtreebooks.com

Crabtree Publishing Company

www.crabtreebooks.com

To Vera and Susan Bailey, for all of their love and support

Coordinating editor: Ellen Rodger
Series editor: Carrie Gleason
Project editor: Rachel Eagen
Editors: Adrianna Morganelli, L. Michelle Nielsen, Jennifer Lackey
Design and production coordinator: Rosie Gowsell
Cover design, layout, and production assistance: Samara Parent
Art direction: Rob MacGregor
Photo research: Allison Napier
Prepress technician: Nancy Johnson

Photo Credits: AA World Travel Library/Alamy: p. 28; Images Etc Ltd/Alamy: p. 25; Zute Lightfoot/Alamy: p. 30; tom schmelzer/Alamy: p. 23 (bottom) Stock Montage, Inc./Alamy: p. 24; Nicolas Sapieha/Art Resource, NY: p. 22; Giraudon, Banco Nacional Ultramarino, Portugal/The Bridgeman Art Library: cover; Museu de Marinha, Lisbon, Portugal/The Bridgeman Art Library: p. 9 (left) The Stapleton Collection, Private Collection/The Bridgeman Art Library: p. 13 (bottom); Tibor Bognár/Corbis: p. 23 (top) Mark A. Johnson/Corbis: p. 11; Massimo Mastrorillo/Corbis: p. 31; John and Lisa Merrill/Corbis: p. 19; Torleif Svensson/Corbis: p. 7 (top left); The Granger Collection: p. 8, p. 15, p. 18, p. 29; Mary Evans Picture Library/The Image Works: p. 12, pp. 16-17; Roger-Viollet/The Image Works: p. 6; Topham/The Image Works: p. 26. Other images from stock CD.

Illustrations: Dennis Gregory Teakle: p. 4; David Wysotski, Allure Illustrations: pp. 20-21

Cartography: Jim Chernishenko: title page, p. 10

Cover: This tapestry from the 1500s portrays the arrival of Vasco da Gama in India on May 20, 1498.

Title page: Vasco da Gama was the first European to reach India by sea. His voyages opened up trade and commerce for his country, Portugal, and the rest of Europe.

Sidebar icon: Arab traders used camels to transport trade items across the overland trade routes of Africa and Asia. Camels could carry large amounts of goods and supplies on their backs, and they could travel far distances without drinking water, even in the desert.

Library and Archives Canada Cataloguing in Publication

Bailey, Katharine, 1980-
   Vasco da Gama : quest for the spice trade / Katharine Bailey.

(In the footsteps of explorers)
Includes index.
ISBN 978-0-7787-2421-6 (bound)
ISBN 978-0-7787-2457-5 (pbk.)

   1. Gama, Vasco da, 1469-1524--Juvenile literature.
2. Explorers--Portugal--Biography--Juvenile literature.
3. India--Discovery and exploration--Portuguese--Juvenile literature.
I. Title. II. Series.

G286.G2B33 2007   j915.404'245092   C2007-900662-0

Library of Congress Cataloging-in-Publication Data

Bailey, Katharine, 1980-
   Vasco da Gama : quest for the spice trade / written by Katharine Bailey.
     p. cm. -- (In the footsteps of explorers)
Includes index.
ISBN-13: 978-0-7787-2421-6 (rlb)
ISBN-10: 0-7787-2421-2 (rlb)
ISBN-13: 978-0-7787-2457-5 (pb)
ISBN-10: 0-7787-2457-3 (pb)
   1. Gama, Vasco da, 1469-1524--Juvenile literature. 2.
Explorers--Portugal--Biography--Juvenile literature. 3. India--Discovery and exploration--Juvenile literature. I. Title. II. Series.

G286.G2B25 2007
915.404'245092--dc22
[B]   2007003407

Crabtree Publishing Company

www.crabtreebooks.com   1-800-387-7650

Published in Canada
Crabtree Publishing
616 Welland Ave.
St. Catharines, ON
L2M 5V6

Published in the United States
Crabtree Publishing
PMB16A
350 Fifth Ave., Suite 3308
New York, NY 10118

Published in the United Kingdom
Crabtree Publishing
White Cross Mills
High Town, Lancaster
LA1 4XS

Published in Australia
Crabtree Publishing
386 Mt. Alexander Rd.
Ascot Vale (Melbourne)
VIC 3032

Contents

The Quest for India

Vasco da Gama was the first European to discover a sea route from Europe to India. His voyage helped launch a new era of discovery and world trade, a period which is now known as the Age of Exploration.

Vasco da Gama was the first European to reach India by sea. The route he navigated opened up trade between Europe and the East. Da Gama's voyages also influenced many explorers who came after him.

A Sea of Change

In the mid-1400s, European nations were eager to find a sea route to India. The Far East, as Europeans referred to India and Southeast Asia, was known for trade items such as gold, silk, and spices. The region could be reached by land, but the route was long and dangerous. It was also controlled by **Arab** traders from the **Middle East** and the north of Africa. If Europeans wanted access to the trade goods of India, they would have to find a way by sea.

In Ship Shape

Ships were an ideal way to transport goods. They could carry more than the **caravans** that were commonly used on overland routes. Travel by sea presented some difficulties. The route to India was unknown, and ocean exploration was expensive and dangerous. Sailors often died of **scurvy**, or they drowned when their ships sank in storms. Despite this, the lure of riches from the East was great, and in 1495, King Manuel I of Portugal decided to send a **fleet** to **navigate** a sea route to India. Vasco da Gama was chosen to lead this **expedition**.

Crew Journal

A member of da Gama's crew kept a journal of da Gama's first voyage to India. The journal, called the *Roteiro*, provided a detailed account of the two-year voyage. The following passage from the *Roteiro* describes the arrival of da Gama's ships in Calicut, the present-day city of Kozhikode in the state of Kerala, India. Da Gama sent a man out to meet with local traders.

The first greeting that he received was in these words: "May the Devil take thee! What brought you hither?" They asked what he sought so far away from home, and he told them that we came in search of **Christians** *and of spices... After this conversation they took him to their lodgings and gave him wheaten bread and honey. When he had eaten he returned to the ships, accompanied by one of the* **Moors**, *who was no sooner on board, than he said these words: "A lucky venture, a lucky venture! Plenty of rubies, plenty of emeralds! You owe great thanks to God, for having brought you to a country holding such riches!"*

(right) Europeans who were eager to make their fortunes sought spices such as cloves, cinnamon, and pepper from the East.

- 1469 -
Da Gama is born in Portugal.

- 1497 to 1499 -
Da Gama's first voyage to India.

- 1502 to 1503 -
Da Gama leads a second voyage to India.

- 1524 -
Da Gama is appointed Viceroy of India.

- 1524 -
Da Gama sails to India, and dies on December 24.

Portugal Explores

The Age of Exploration began in the 1400s. Portugal led the way with advanced shipbuilding, fearless captains, and enthusiasm for ocean travel.

An Ongoing Battle

Portugal is part of the Iberian Peninsula in southwestern Europe. In the 700s, **Moors**, or **Muslims** from North Africa, conquered the Iberian Peninsula. Over time, the Portuguese recaptured Lisbon, which later became the capital city of Portugal. The Moors and the Portuguese, who were **Christian**, continued to fight over territory. Religious differences heightened the tension between the two groups of people.

To the Sea!

By the early 1400s, the Portuguese were having conflicts with other groups of Muslims as well. Muslim merchants from Arabia controlled Europe's trade with distant lands in the East. These merchants bought valuable items such as spices and silk in the Middle East, India, and China. They took the items to Europe and sold them for a much higher price. The Portuguese wanted to go to the places where these things came from and buy the items directly for a lower price. The Arab merchants who controlled all the overland trade routes would not allow the Portuguese to go through, so the Portuguese turned to the sea to find another route to the East.

(background) Bartolomeu Dias helped da Gama's voyages by reaching the Cape of Good Hope.

(above) Arab traders brought trade items across the desert using long trains of camels. These caravans, as they were called, were also useful in hauling supplies, including food and water.

Discovery

Prince Henry of Portugal, nicknamed "the Navigator" for his pursuit of ocean exploration, began sponsoring, or funding, sea expeditions. He wanted to find a route to India, where he knew spices and other valuable items were traded. Portuguese expeditions explored the west coast of Africa, trading for gold and other items. The Portuguese explorers claimed new territory, such as the island of Madeira off Africa's northwest coast, but none of the expeditions went as far as India. A breakthrough occurred when Portuguese explorer Bartolomeu Dias rounded the southern tip of Africa in 1488. His sailors were terrified of the **uncharted** waters, but Dias pressed on, sailing through what was later named the Cape of Good Hope. After rounding the tip, Dias turned back and returned to Europe.

-1415-
The Portuguese capture the city of Ceuta.

- 1425 -
Madeira is discovered and settled.

- 1488 -
Bartolomeu Dias sails around the southern tip of Africa.

- 1492 -
Christopher Columbus claims the Caribbean for Spain.

Young da Gama

Vasco da Gama grew up in the small coastal town of Sines, Portugal. He was the son of a noble, and was educated in mathematics and navigation. Historians believe he learned to love the ocean by listening to the tales of sailors who landed at his seaside village.

The da Gama Family

Vasco da Gama was born around 1469 to his father Estêvão and his mother Isabelle. His exact birth date is not known. Little is known of Vasco da Gama's early life, but historians believe that because he was the son of a noble, he was given a good education, served in the army, and was granted opportunities to sail on trade voyages to Africa.

A Task Accomplished

In 1492, a French crew seized and looted a Portuguese ship on a return trip from Africa. The ship carried a valuable cargo of gold. King John II of Portugal **retaliated** by ordering Vasco da Gama to seize all of the French ships in Portuguese ports. Da Gama captured the ships and collected all the goods onboard. Da Gama's skill in this incident impressed the king, earning da Gama a **reputation** for fearless leadership.

(right) Vasco da Gama departs for India.

Set to Sail

King John II died in 1495, and his brother-in-law and cousin, Manuel I, became king. The new king immediately appointed Vasco da Gama as **commander** of an expedition of four ships to India. Ships were built and packed with great stores of **provisions**. Barrels of wine and water were filled, and food and weapons were stored in the ships' cargo holds. A crew of 180 men was hired, including Vasco da Gama's brother Paulo, who was captain of one of the ships.

Trading Expeditions

Ships on trading expeditions were stocked with items that could be traded along the way for valuable goods, food, and water. Some trade goods were given to the local peoples as gifts as a way of establishing good intentions with the people encountered in new places. For reasons unknown, King Manuel gave da Gama very few items of worth to trade on the voyage. European gifts such as coral beads and honey were not valued by the rich rulers in Africa and India. Some historians believe King Manual did not think da Gama's expedition would return, so he did not bother sending along valuable trade items. Without valuable trade items, da Gama was not properly prepared to meet the rulers of India.

(above) King John II encouraged sea exploration for trade purposes.

- 1492 -
Da Gama seizes French ships for King John II.

- 1495 -
Manuel I becomes Portugal's king.

- 1495 -
Vasco da Gama is chosen to command an expedition to India.

Reaching India

Vasco da Gama sailed from Portugal on July 8, 1497. The purpose of his voyage was to discover the sea route to India to access the riches there.

South by West

The fleet left the port of Lisbon and sailed south. They passed the Spanish-controlled Canary Islands, and continued to the Portuguese colony at the Cape Verde Islands, where the ships restocked with supplies. The fleet continued, using the **prevailing winds** to chart a southwest course, which brought them close to South America. The ships headed back east at the Tropic of Capricorn, an invisible line that stretches east and west around the world, just below the equator. This course used the natural winds and ocean currents to speed up their journey.

Da Gama's first voyage 1497-1499: →→

Da Gama's second voyage 1502-1503: →→

Da Gama's third voyage 1524: →→

EUROPE

ASIA

Lisbon

Arabia

India

Goa

Calicut

Cochin

AFRICA

Cape Verde Islands

Malindi

Mombasa

Mozambique

Indian Ocean

St. Helena Bay

Natal

Atlantic Ocean

Cape of Good Hope

Sailing Past The Cape

The ships sailed toward South Africa, stopping briefly in an area that da Gama named St. Helena Bay. The fleet then sailed around the southern tip of Africa, called the Cape of Good Hope.

Mozambique

The fleet sailed north, dropping anchor off the coast of what is today Mozambique. The ships were in bad repair and the crew needed fresh water. The crew traded with a group of local people who also gave them fresh water. After repairing the ships, da Gama's fleet sailed north until they landed at Mozambique Island. Da Gama hired two **pilots** there to help navigate the rest of the journey. He did not want the Muslim people who lived there to know that the crew was Christian. Relations between the two groups soured when the people of the island learned that the Portuguese were Christian. Da Gama's crew attacked the people with cannon and guns before departing.

(background) The clash of the Atlantic and Indian oceans at the Cape of Good Hope creates powerful waves and currents that can sink ships. Da Gama's crew begged him to turn around, but he pressed on.

Dangerous Waters

Word of the assault on Mozambique traveled ahead of Vasco da Gama as he sailed north. At each port they entered, the fleet was treated with suspicion. Their journey grew riskier as it became harder to find safe ports for food, water, and repairs.

Arrival in Mombasa

The guides hired at Mozambique Island tricked the Portuguese into sailing into rocky waters. The fleet struggled to sail north but was hindered by storms and shallow waters. The ships finally anchored at Mombasa, a large and busy trading port on the east coast of Africa.

Attacked by Night

The people of Mombasa had heard of the attack on Mozambique Island and sought revenge. That night, da Gama's fleet was swarmed. Da Gama's crew defended themselves, but after a second attack the following day, they set sail. Shortly after leaving Mombasa, da Gama spotted three ships at sea. He ordered his men to seize and loot the ships, which carried cargoes of gold and silver, along with food and water. Everyone onboard was taken hostage.

(below) Ten criminals were brought from Portugal on da Gama's voyage to do unpleasant and dangerous duties that the rest of the crew did not want to do, such as going ashore in unknown ports.

Malindi

The fleet next stopped at the Muslim port of Malindi. Da Gama was worried about being attacked again, so he did not want to go ashore. He sent a message to the ruler of Malindi that he was under strict orders from the king of Portugal not to go ashore. He sent gifts to the ruler of Malindi and released the prisoners he had captured near Mombasa to establish a good relationship. The ruler of Malindi provided da Gama with a guide to help them navigate to India, and the fleet departed.

First To India

The fleet sailed across the Indian Ocean, propelled by the summer **monsoon** winds. The Malindi guide was very helpful. After 23 days at sea, the fleet landed on the beach of Kappakadavu, north of Calicut, or the present-day city of Kozhikode in the state of Kerala, India. Da Gama and his crew were the first Europeans to reach India by sea.

Stories about sea monsters in unfamiliar waters terrified sailors. Some of da Gama's crew thought they would not return to Europe alive.

- July 8, 1497 -
Da Gama's fleet departs for India.

- May 20, 1498 -
Da Gama arrives in Calicut.

- February, 1502 -
Da Gama departs for his second voyage to India.

- October 1, 1502 -
Da Gama sinks the *Mîrî*.

- October 10, 1503 -
Da Gama's fleet arrives home in Portugal.

Calicut: Port of Spices

Calicut was one of the richest and busiest trading centers in India. Hundreds of boats waited in the harbor to trade spices, gold, expensive fabrics, and gems.

First Contact

Da Gama sent a crew member named João Nunes, who spoke the Arabic language, ashore to greet the local peoples. The port thrived with traders from the East, the **Mediterranean**, and Africa. Two languages were common in Calicut. Hindi was the language spoken by the local Indian people, and Arabic was spoken by the Arab traders. Nunes discovered that the ruler of Calicut lived in a small village farther south. The ruler was called the Zamorin. Zamorin is an **anglicized** version of the Hindi term Samoothirippadu, or Samoothiri, which means ruler. Da Gama dressed in his finest clothing and set out to meet the Zamorin in hopes of reaching a trade agreement in Calicut.

The Gifts are Refused

Da Gama went ashore to meet with the Zamorin. Da Gama's gifts of striped fabric and coral beads were inspected by one of the Zamorin's men, who said the gifts were so poor they were insulting. He forbade da Gama from giving them to the Zamorin. Da Gama presented the Zamorin with letters from King Manuel, requesting a trade agreement between the Portuguese and the merchants at Calicut. The Zamorin was displeased, as he was used to receiving lavish gifts from traders to his city, and he had expected gold. He refused to approve a trading agreement and told da Gama to leave Calicut immediately.

(top and left) Spices such as pepper and cinnamon were expensive in Europe, and selling them there could mean huge profits. They were lightweight and did not spoil over long voyages.

Departure

Da Gama sailed from Calicut in August. The winter monsoon winds, which would help push the fleet onward, had not yet arrived. The journey home took three long months, during which over 100 of the crew died. Half of the fleet returned to Portugal on July 10, 1499, two years after their departure. Da Gama was delayed when his brother Paulo became ill and died in the Azores, a group of islands off the coast of Portugal. Da Gama mourned his brother before returning home.

The Triumph of Return

King Manuel was extremely pleased when da Gama returned. Portugal was able to claim rights to the lands da Gama had visited. The small cargoes of spices and goods the ships brought back were enough to cover the cost of the voyage. Da Gama was given two **pensions**, and granted the title of Dom, which signified his high **status**. He was named **Admiral** of India, which entitled him to lead future expeditions. Da Gama married, and settled in Sines.

(background) An artist's depiction of da Gama's first meeting with the Zamorin of Calicut shows a large crowd of curious local people. The crowd grew so large that several people were trampled in the crush of bodies.

Turmoil in India

Vasco da Gama sailed to India for a second time in 1502. The purpose of the expedition was to assert a dominant Portuguese presence in the spice trade. What da Gama could not get through trade, he took through violence.

Da Gama Returns to India

In 1502, King Manuel selected da Gama to lead another expedition to India. This time da Gama's fleet included 20 ships. Da Gama sailed around Africa, to the port of Kilwa in Mozambique. He anchored off the coast and sent several messages ashore requesting to see Kilwa's ruler, Amir Ibrahim. The messages were not returned until da Gama threatened to bombard the port with cannon fire. Da Gama demanded that the ruler of Kilwa give the Portuguese a gift of gold and declare allegiance to Portugal by planting Portugal's flag on their shores. Ibrahim agreed, and da Gama's fleet set sail for Calicut.

(background) Vasco da Gama's fleet sailed into unknown waters and faced many dangers at sea, including strong currents and storms. The biggest threat to da Gama's crew was not the sea, but illnesses such as scurvy.

The *Mîrî*

Before arriving in Calicut, da Gama decided to capture a passing merchant ship for its cargo. He found a ship called the *Mîrî* carrying about 300 of Calicut's richest merchants. They were returning from Mecca, a Muslim holy city in present-day Saudi Arabia. Da Gama fired at the ship and demanded its surrender. The *Mîrî's* captain tried to trade the goods onboard for his people's lives, but da Gama wanted more valuable items than those onboard. Da Gama's crew set the ship on fire, killing everyone aboard. It is not known what prompted such a vicious attack. Some historians believe that da Gama was trying to scare anyone who might want to keep Portugal from taking over the trade routes to the East.

Calicut Bombarded

Da Gama was welcomed by the Zamorin in Calicut, but da Gama kidnapped and killed 38 Calicut fishermen in revenge for his treatment during his last voyage. His ships then sailed south to another Portuguese trading post in Cochin, now known as Kochi, India. They traded there for three months before the Zamorin of Calicut lured da Gama back. The Muslim fleet attacked da Gama's ships when they reached the harbor. Da Gama responded by killing a young Calicut man and hanging his body from the ship's mast. A battle broke out. By the time da Gama left, he had proved that the Portuguese would do great violence to get what they wanted. He had also amassed a large cargo of spices, silks, gold, and gems.

Disaster in India

Before da Gama returned to India, Portuguese explorer Pedro Àlvares Cabral led an expedition that reached Calicut in September 1500. Cabral wanted permission for a permanent Portuguese trading post in Calicut. The Zamorin agreed. This angered the Arab merchants who had been buying goods in Calicut and selling them in Europe for hundreds of years. A bloody battle broke out between the Portuguese and Arabs that left over 400 dead. Cabral went to Cochin, India, and loaded his ships with spices and silks. They returned to Lisbon in 1501.

Fame and Fortune

Da Gama's first and second voyages made him rich and famous. He was a hero in Portugal but he was not given title to his hometown of Sines as King Manuel had promised. This made da Gama bitter and angry.

Portugal in India

Da Gama's voyages made King Manuel very wealthy. He rewarded da Gama with gifts of money. Da Gama built lavish homes for his wife and seven children in Sines. But the Duke who ruled over Sines did not want to give the town away. King Manuel named da Gama the Count of the Vidiguira region of Portugal instead. Da Gama moved his family there. During this time, several Portuguese **fortifications** were built along the west coast of India and a **colony** was established at the present-day state of Goa, north of Calicut.

(background) This engraving shows a market scene from the colony at Goa. Portuguese soldiers killed thousands of local people as they dominated the area.

Third Expedition

King Manuel died of the **plague** in 1521, leaving the throne to his son João III. King João chose Vasco da Gama to lead another expedition to India. His orders were to investigate what was happening at Portuguese ports, where many of the governors placed in charge were more interested in gaining personal wealth than they were in building a Portuguese **empire**. Da Gama agreed to the voyage on the condition that he be named the new **Viceroy** of India. His request was granted, and the new title gave him control over Portugal's ports in India.

The Last Voyage

Da Gama's fleet left Lisbon, Portugal, and reached India in September 1524. Da Gama's orders were to replace the **corrupt** governors of the trading ports in the region. Da Gama's rule in India was short-lived. After residing in Goa for three months, da Gama became sick with an unknown disease. Da Gama moved on to Cochin to try to resume his role as viceroy, but his health deteriorated. Vasco da Gama died on December 24, 1524. He was buried in Cochin at the Portuguese church of Santo Antonio.

What Happened to the Body?

Vasco da Gama's adventures continued after his death. After his burial at Cochin, his body was moved back to Portugal and buried in Vidigueira. He remained there until 1880, when his body was transferred to the Monastery of Jeronimos at Belem. This monastery outside Lisbon was built by King Manuel in 1502 to give thanks to God for the success of da Gama's first voyage. In the 1880s, it was realized that the wrong body had been moved! Vasco da Gama's body was finally moved to Belem in 1898, and it remains there today.

Vasco da Gama reached his final resting place over 300 years after his death.

Life at Sea

Vasco da Gama's ocean voyages were long, dangerous, and filled with uncertainty. The ships had to be strong enough to withstand huge waves and fierce ocean storms.

The Nau

The Portuguese were expert shipbuilders. A new, larger design, called the nau, was made for the India expeditions. Naus featured large hulls made of smooth, interlocking wooden panels. Hulls were painted with black tar to help prevent leaks and protect the wood from the salt water of the oceans. The ships had two to four masts, with a combination of square and lateen, or triangular, sails.

Navigation

Pilots could direct ships by using the stars or a **compass**. Another method of navigation was called dead reckoning. The pilot figured out the ship's position by estimating how fast the ship had been going. Then he could compare his guess of the ship's position to maps. None of these methods were very accurate. Only very skilled pilots could get their ships safely to their destinations.

Da Gama's fleet was battle-ready. Weapons, such as crossbows, were stocked in the cargo hold below the main deck.

Millet Porridge

Porridge was a common seafaring food because the dry grain used to make it did not spoil on long journeys. Millet porridge was also popular in the parts of Africa and India that Vasco da Gama explored. Here is a simple recipe to try. Ask an adult for help.

Ingredients:
1/2 cup (125 mL) millet
3 cups (710 mL) water
1/4 teaspoon (1.2 mL) salt
1 handful currants or raisins
3 tablespoons (45 mL) slivered almonds, toasted in a small skillet
Butter or sour cream

Directions:
1. Rinse the millet.
2. Bring the water to a boil.
3. Add the salt, millet, and currants or raisins, then simmer over low heat for 30 minutes.
4. Top with slivered almonds and a pat of butter or sour cream.

(right) Grains such as millet were ideal at sea because they did not spoil.

(background) Da Gama's crews were divided by rank. The captain was in charge of commanding the crew, with the help of supervising officers. The pilot plotted the ship's course, while the surgeon carried out basic medical procedures, such as pulling rotten teeth and dressing wounds. Ship's boys were usually young boys who scrubbed decks and cleaned up after meals.

India's Trading Ports

The trading ports of southern India hummed with activity when da Gama arrived in 1498. Merchants from Asia and Africa were eager to make their fortunes by trading for spices, silk and other fine fabrics, and gold.

A History of Change

India is home to some of the oldest civilizations in the world. Around 3600 B.C., people began settling the city of Harappa along the Indus River Valley, a region in present-day Pakistan and north-western India. Around 700 A.D., Muslims from Central Asia invaded India. Turks arrived in the 1100s and ruled the region. By the time the Portuguese arrived, India was a place of many religions, languages, and cultures.

Rulers

At the time of da Gama's expeditions, southern India was ruled by a Hindu **dynasty** called the Vijayanagar. The dynasty's rulers were focused on trading and they grew wealthy. Calicut was part of their empire and the Zamorin collected taxes from the local merchants on behalf of the ruling family.

(above) The remains of a Vijayanagar dynasty Hindu temple.

Religion

In the 1400s, India was dominated by two main religions: **Islam** and **Hinduism**. Islam was the religion of the Arab merchants and Hinduism was the religion of the local Indian people. Followers of Islam are called Muslims and they believe in one god, Allah. Hindus have many different gods and believe that people are reborn in new bodies after they die.

Many Muslim mosques, or places of worship, like this one in northern India, have courtyards, arched doorways, minaret towers, and domes.

The People of Calicut

When da Gama arrived, the Hindu people of Calicut did not wear a lot of clothing because it is very hot in India. Both men and women wore pieces of cotton tied around their waists. They grew their hair long and tied it in intricate knots. Wealthy people wore jewelry of gold and silver, while poorer people wore jewelry of tin and glass beads. Their homes were made of adobe, a mixture of water, clay, and straw.

A man sells flowers near a Hindu temple. He wears simple cotton clothing much like that worn by the residents of Calicut in the 1500s.

Trading in Calicut

Calicut was one of the biggest and busiest ports in India. Large warehouses were constructed along the waterfront and a **bazaar** was built nearby, where merchants were allowed to store their goods while traveling to and from their homelands. Guards patrolled the warehouse area and bazaar at all times to prevent theft.

Tax and Trade

The Zamorin collected port duties from merchants who traded in Calicut. Duties were paid in exchange for the use of port warehouses and bazaars. During da Gama's first visit to Calicut, he refused to pay port duties. This contributed to the poor relationship between the Zamorin and the Portuguese.

The Spice Trade

Vasco da Gama's journeys helped Portugal uncover the spice trade of the East. The Portuguese had known that spices came from the East, but traders were secretive about where the spices came from. Muslim traders who had a **monopoly** on the spice markets of the East did not want it broken. In Calicut, da Gama and his crew learned not only where spices came from, but also how they passed along sea routes and overland trade routes. This knowledge later helped Portugal establish fortifications in Africa and India to dominate the spice trade.

Unlike other traders, da Gama refused to pay the port duties or taxes. Port duties paid for the guards to patrol and prevent theft.

The Bazaar's Beginnings

It was said that a wealthy merchant trading in Calicut once had so much gold that he worried that his ships would sink from the weight. He left a large crate of gold with the Zamorin to pick up later, but he thought it would probably be stolen while he was gone. When he returned months later, the gold was still there. He offered the Zamorin half of the gold as a reward for his honesty. The Zamorin refused, saying he was only doing his duty as the ruler of the city. So instead, the merchant founded the Calicut bazaar in thanks.

(background) Spice sellers still ply their trade in Indian bazaars. Calicut was a busy trading port when da Gama came to India.

Portugal's Empire

Vasco da Gama's discovery of a sea route to India had a major impact on Portugal and the rest of the world. The Portuguese set up colonies in India and Africa, and established a monopoly over the spice trade in the Indian Ocean.

Hunger for More

Da Gama's voyages began a period of about 100 years in which Portugal controlled the major ocean trading routes of the East. The Portuguese came to dominate trade in ports along the east coast of Africa and the west coast of India. Portuguese settlements were built at Mozambique, Zanzibar, and Hormuz in Africa, Mumbai in India, Ceylon in present-day Sri Lanka, Macao in China, and Malacca in Malaysia. The Portuguese often treated the local people in their colonies with brutality and violence.

A European tapestry from the 1500s shows da Gama's arrival in Calicut. Da Gama's entry into India was the beginning of Portuguese and European expansion.

Plantations

Many Portuguese colonies had large farms called plantations. Colony plantations often grew a single crop that did not grow well in the colder, drier climates of Europe, like sugar or tea. By owning the plantations themselves, the Portuguese did not have to pay local farmers. They got expensive goods at a cheap price.

Slavery

Slaves from Africa were the main source of workers on plantations. Slaves were people who were forced through violence and mistreatment to work for no pay. They were often kidnapped from their homes and sold to other people by **slave traders**. As the Portuguese expanded their empire, the number of plantations increased. The number of slaves needed to work the plantations grew and more people were kidnapped from their homes in Africa to fill the need for workers.

- April 9, 1524 -
Da Gama sails to India for the third time.

- September 23, 1524 -
The fleet arrives in Goa, India.

- November 1524 -
Da Gama moves from Goa to Cochin.

- December 24, 1524 -
Da Gama dies in Cochin, India.

The Portuguese planted sugar cane at their colonies, and used slaves to grow and harvest it. Once processed, the sugar was shipped to Europe. Plantation owners made huge profits this way.

The Price to Pay

Portugal's explosion into world trade, along with the claiming of new territory, put a strain on the small country. Thousands of Portuguese men left their farms, homes, and families to seek their fortunes in spices overseas. Many died on the dangerous route to India. So many people left their farms that food shortages became common in Portuguese cities. As the empire expanded, Portugal no longer had enough people or money to protect its forts and ships. This made them vulnerable to attacks and they started losing their monopoly on trade from the mid-1500s onwards.

The Portuguese began building ships that could sail great distances beginning in the late 1400s. This image shows a caravel, a small ship with many sails, depicted in tiles.

The Rest of Europe Catches Up

Vasco da Gama's discovery of a sea route around Africa started a race between European nations to claim new lands and discover new sea routes. Spain became Portugal's biggest rival and eventually became a larger and more important empire than Portugal. Later, first the Dutch and then the British dominated the trade routes. By the 1850s, Great Britain alone ruled over most of the Indian subcontinent.

(background) The British Prince of Wales, son of the Queen of England, enters an Indian city on the top of a decorated elephant in 1875. After gaining control of trade routes, once dominated by Portugal and other European countries, Britain ruled India for almost one hundred years. India gained independence in 1947.

Vasco da Gama's Legacy

Many people in Portugal think of Vasco da Gama as a hero. His discoveries helped Portugal become a powerful, wealthy nation. Da Gama is not as kindly remembered in other parts of the world, such as India, where his brutal and violent acts caused many deaths.

Colonialism

Portugal and other European nations often brought misery to the places they colonized. The natives of colonized areas were brutally murdered by European conquerers or fell ill with diseases brought by European colonists. They often lost conrol of their lands and were enslaved to feed a growing European desire for goods from around the world. Because of this legacy of violence and despair, in 1998, many people in India protested the government's plans to commemorate the 500th anniversary of da Gama's landing in Calicut. Those people believed that da Gama's arrival was nothing to celebrate.

After his death, da Gama statues were erected in several places he stopped along his voyages. This one is on Mozambique Island.

The Legend of Da Gama

The da Gama name survives in many monuments to the explorer's determination. Vasco da Gama is the largest city in Goa, India. The Vasco da Gama bridge crosses the Tagus River in Lisbon, and a street is named after him in Sines. His memory is evoked by a Portuguese epic poem written in 1572 called *Os Lusiadas*, or *The Lusiads*, which is based on his experiences. Vasco da Gama is the lead character in Giacomo Meyerbeer's opera *L'Africaine*. There is even a crater on the moon named after Vasco da Gama.

The World Remembers

The 500th anniversary of Vasco da Gama's landing in India was celebrated in 1998, when Portugal hosted the **World's Fair**, or Expo '98. The theme of the event was to celebrate Portuguese exploration and it coincided with the 500th anniversary of da Gama's arrival in Calicut, India. One of the highlights of Expo '98 was the opening of the Vasco da Gama bridge in Lisbon. The bridge spans for 11 miles (17 kilometers). It is one of the longest bridges in Europe.

(background) *The Vasco da Gama bridge is cable-stayed, which means that strong cables stretch from supporting pillars to hold up the road.*

Glossary

Admiral A high rank in the navy that places a person in charge of a fleet of ships

anglicized Made to sound like an English word

Arab An ethnic group that originated in the Middle East

bazaar A market where goods are bought and sold

caravans Large groups of traders that traveled aross deserts carrying supplies on the backs of camels

Christian A follower of the teachings of Jesus Christ, whom Christians believe is God's son

colony Land ruled by another nation

commander An officer with authority over others

compass A device that uses a magnet to show which direction is north

corrupt Dishonest

dynasty A succession of rulers from the same family

empire A large area under the control of one person or nation

expedition A long voyage with specific goals

fleet A group of ships

fortifications Places surrounded by protective walls

Hinduism An ancient religion of India

Islam A religion whose followers believe in one god and the teachings of the prophet Muhammad

Mediterranean Land bordering the Mediterranean Sea, including countries such as Spain, France, Monaco, and Italy

Middle East A region that lies to the east and south of the Mediterranean Sea

monopoly Exclusive rights to trade specific goods within one region

monsoon A weather system that brings rain from May to September and dryness from October to April. Monsoons affect India and Southeast Asia

Moors Muslims from North Africa

Muslims People who follow the religion of Islam

navigate To find or direct a route, usually by sea

noble A person of high rank in society in the 1400s

pensions Regular payments made to someone

pilots People who help others navigate through an area that is unfamiliar to them

plague A fatal disease

port A seaside town with a harbor where ships dock

prevailing winds Seasonal winds that blow from a certain direction

provisions Supplies

reputation How a person is thought of by others

retaliated Sought revenge for something

scurvy A painful disease resulting from lack of vitamin C. It blackens gums and causes teeth to fall out. It is lethal if not treated

slave traders People who buy or capture slaves and sell them to other people

status Someone's place in society

title Rights to a property

uncharted Unmapped or unfamiliar

Viceroy The representative of the king or queen who rules a territory as governor

World's Fair An exhibition where many countries display their scientific, technological, and artistic achievements

Index

Printed in the U.S.A.